Parenting is WONDER-full

Sue Miller

& Holly Delich

Design: Ryan Carroll

Parenting is Wonder-full
Published by Orange, a division of The reThink Group, Inc.
5870 Charlotte Lane, Suite 300
Cumming, GA 30040 U.S.A.

The Orange logo is a registered trademark of The reThink Group, Inc.

Other Orange products are available online and direct from the publisher. Visit our website at www.WhatIsOrange.org for more resources like these.

ISBN: 978-0-9854116-0-2

©2012 The reThink Group, Inc.

Writers: Holly Delich and Sue Miller
The reThink Group Editing Team: Ryan Boon, Jennifer Davis, Kathy Hill, Lois Pallansch, Dan Scott
Design: Ryan Carroll

Printed in the United States of America
First Edition 2012

1 2 3 4 5 6 7 8 9 10

04/04/12

There is no book on how to do this

(Even though this is a book on how to do this)

Christina Jankins @CJWWing
View Your Profile

1126	225	105
TWEETS	FOLLOWING	FOLLOWERS

Compose New Tweet...

Edde Campbell @Edde26 2min
Putting them on a schedule is so important. Remember, it's #EatPlaySleep

Neve Darnell @neved8 4min
Let them create their own schedule.

Sandra Everleigh @sanever 10min
Never let them nap in the car. Don't ever co-sleep.

Eden Hayes @edenhayes123 14min
Co-sleeping is the only way to get them to sleep.

Jimmy O'Dell @dudeurgettinodell 16min
Don't ever let them sleep on their tummy.

Sara McNally @nallyMC 18min
Make sure they have tummy time.

Elizabeth Carol @carol83
Use cloth diapers, it's not that much of a hassle.

Sara McNally @nallyMC
@carol8316 Disposable diape are the way to go! #ThrowAw

Eden Hayes @edenhayes1
@carol8316 Organic diapers a far better for the environment

Sandra Everleigh @sanev
If your child sleeps in another room it can cause SIDS!

David Candler @daveyc3
SIDS? What is that?!?!

Edde Campbell @Edde26
Crib bumpers can cause SIDS #DontUseEm

Eden Hayes @edenhayes1
I've heard SIDS can be cause by stuffed animals.

Neve Darnell @neved8
WE DON'T KNOW WHAT CAU SIDS!

25min	**Sandra Everleigh** @sanever	1hr
	Baby's not sleeping. I think it's colic	

28min	**Eden Hayes** @edenhayes123	1hr
	@sanever It's reflux.	

28min	**Jimmy O'Dell** @dudeurgettinodell	2hr
	@sanever It's just gas.	

29min	**Edde Campbell** @Edde26	2hr
	@sanever It's teething.	

30min	**Elizabeth Carol** @carol8316	2hr
	@sanever It's chicken pox.	

38min	**Neve Darnell** @neved8	3hr
	@sanever It's thrush.	

45min	**David Candler** @daveyc3po	3hr
	@sanever It's hand, foot and mouth. #StayAway	

58min	**Christina Jankins** @CJWWing	4hr
	@sanever Don't go to the ER, they'll catch something else.	

milkshakes

copious amounts
of "reality" TV

confusion

anxiety
medication

Which May Lead You To This...

self-doubt

late night calls
to your mother

putting your
pediatrician on
speed dial

uncontrollable
sobbing

This is Jessie.

She nursed till she was three. She is now a Marine Biologist.

This is Peyton.

She lived on Cheetos and Flintstone vitamins. She graduated Suma Cum Laude.

This is Steven.

He slept on his parents floor until he was nine. He doesn't do that anymore.

Take Heart...

This is Rocky.

The only way he would use the potty is backwards so he could play army men on the tank. He is now married with kids of his own.

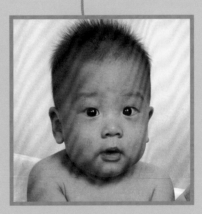

This is Lee.

He refused to touch a vegetable until he was five. He now runs an organic farm.

This is Mya.

During preschool testing, she identified all numbers as the letter "P." She just won "Teacher of the Year."

Re-Read page 5 and

BRE

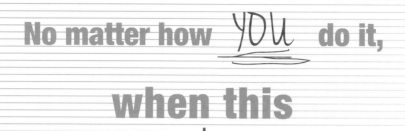

No matter how *you* do it,

when this

happens to *you*

You'll begin
to
WONDER
things you
never
did
before.

HAVE YOU EVER WONDERED

how you could love this much?

"A baby will make love stronger, days shorter, nights longer, bankroll smaller, a home happier, clothes shabbier, the past forgotten and the future worth living for."

A baby's brain will double in the first year to become half of its overall size.

Babies are born with 300 bones. Adults have 206.

Marvelously Made

Babies can recognize their mother at birth by her voice and smell.

Newborns can hear as well as you.

Babies can see 8 to 15 inches away— the perfect distance to be able to see the face of whoever is feeding them.

Babies born in May are the heaviest on average.

Babies can determine where a sound is coming from 10 minutes after being born.

Touch is one of baby's most advanced senses at birth.

Babies have no tears until week three.

This is Maggie. Her Mommy calls her "Princess"—though as a newborn, "Diva" might have been a better nickname. Her Mama puts it like this:

Sleep.

That's what a new mother needs.

Sleep.

And a handbook, a new parent handbook that actually interprets the cries and tells you EXACTLY what they mean.

That would be wonderful.

I can remember one afternoon not long after my princess was born.

I was exhausted, and a friend had come over to help.

However, Miss Princess wasn't interested in any help.

She wasn't interested in anything we had to offer.

She just lay there and cried and cried and cried.

And screamed and screamed and screamed.

We tried a paci. Didn't work.

We tried rocking. Didn't work.

We tried a bottle. Didn't work.

We changed her diaper. Didn't work.

We tried bouncing, jiggling, burping, hopping. Didn't work.

She just lay there and cried and cried and cried.

And screamed and screamed and screamed.

My friend, who didn't have children of her own at the time, looked at me with a face filled with complete terror (I'm sure mirroring my own) and screeched, "What do we do now?"

My equally screeched response, "I DON'T KNOW! It's not like I have a baby handbook I'm not sharing with you!"

Yes, a handbook or a translator. That would be awesome.

Miss Princess finally fell asleep.

As I watched her sweet sleeping face and counted her tiny fingers, my terror was replaced by an overwhelming love for the amazing gift I'd been given.

A gift that was worth all the sleep deprivation in the world.

I had become a Mother.

BABIES MAKE

This is Jon and Sunny's daughter Dora. When she was about two years old, they decided to have her dedicated. This is Jon's account of that special day:

While we were loading Dora into the car, I had a miraculous, almost prophetic moment.

I said to my wife, "Hey, let's wait to put Dora's dress on her until we get to the church. You know, to keep her from getting it dirty."

And, in a moment of enlightenment, my wife agreed.

We headed down to the church where countless friends and family awaited. Little did I know, something horrendous was happening in the carseat behind us. Something so mind-blowingly unexpected, that, when I saw it, my eyes literally refused to let my brain understand what it was I was looking at.

Eventually, I managed to produce a tiny, very subtle, blood curdling SCREAM OF HORROR!

Apparently, my daughter had "filled her diaper" during the drive. And, had proceeded to PLAY WITH IT. She was covered from head to toe.

Immediately, my wife and I flew into panic mode. She grabbed Dora's clean dress and ran for the church door like an Olympic sprinter. That left me to pick up the filthy child. I gripped her with my fingertips. I held her as far from me as possible lest I defile myself as well. I carried her into the nearest bathroom where I proceeded to bathe her in a sink.

After using every paper towel I could find and covering myself in so much water it looked like I had stopped to take a dip in the baptismal myself, my daughter was clean. She was in her dress, and ready to be dedicated. And—

It was beautiful.

You'll find that no matter how horrific or difficult a situation can be with your children, it only takes a moment to completely forget how you almost dry-heaved yourself to death and to remember how much you love them. That day was one of those moments.

LOVE STRONGER

This is Erinleigh and her adorable family. You know how they say that truth is stranger than fiction? Well, EL's first few months of motherhood definitely could be made into a LifeTime movie of the week. This is how she tells the tale:

My husband, George, and I wanted to make sure we had "everything" when we were preparing for our first son, Eli. Everything we thought we needed was set up, put up, decorated, and ready a few weeks before Eli entered the world.

Eli made it onto the scene with a little bit of drama, but after seven days in the hospital, we were blessed to bring our healthy little boy home to his impeccably prepared environment. Less than 24 hours after the homecoming, a friend brought us a meal.

We turned on our gas stove to warm the dinner and we discovered that unbeknownst to us, another "helpful" individual had been in our midst. While we were in the hospital, several out-of-town family members and friends had been in our home sleeping, cleaning, and putting plastic cutting boards in the broiler tray . . . of our gas stove . . . on top of the pilot light. As only a new momma can, I smelled gas from across the house. And smoke. I C-section-shuffled into the kitchen to find my mom and George debating whether they should open the oven door and toss flour on the flames or not.

Free tip: Giving oxygen to a build up of gas is not recommended. We do not recommend combining flour with a gas fire either. Actually no one recommends that.

Within seconds our house was filled with screams, flour, and George moving faster than I have ever seen him move in order to save Apple products. When you have been fileted like a fish and haven't pooped in a week, you can only move so fast. But when your sweet little baby is in danger, you will be surprised to know that Olympic records can be

BABIES MAKE

broken. I grabbed Eli and C-section-sprinted outside. Our meal-bearing friend grabbed the car seat and diaper bag. My mom grabbed an armful of clothes and my purse. And proudly, my husband was able to save every electronic that wasn't mounted to the wall or over 300 pounds.

So, there I was. Standing on the sidewalk, holding my son a little too tight, sobbing, and surrounded by electronics as smoke poured from every crevice of our beautiful, perfectly prepared home. Our friend offered to let us stay at her house for the night. One night turned into three months.

Because I was unable to go up and down the stairs, I spent all day alone in a bedroom with my sweet son. Eli slept in a basket on a table. We changed him on a dresser and bathed him on a counter in the bathroom. We dried bottles on a stereo, cleaned dishes in the tub, and made rattles out of ribbon and sticks. And—it was perfect. Looking back, I would not trade those close quarters and quality time for the world.

No matter what your home is like when you add a new little one—if they are your first or your fifth—or if your house burns down, remember that the environment isn't in the stuff or the space. The peace isn't in knowing how you've "got" everything. What you feel when you gaze at that little wonder gurgling in a basket, that's all you need. I was prepared for a lot, but I wasn't prepared to make room in my heart for that much love. And, that love is all they need. It's kind of a perfect situation.

HAVE YOU EVER WONDERED

why this is so hard?

This is Lisa. A single mom with two adopted daughters who give her a run for her money. When her daughter, Angela, was three (the one making the scrunchy face in the picture), she developed a thing for spitting, and Lisa had an inventive solution. She talks about it here:

Someone had recently given me 50 baby food jars to use for art projects at school and they gave me an idea for a plan. After my next drenching, I told Angela how great she was at spraying spit and bet her she couldn't fill a baby food jar with it. She had the time of her life proving me wrong.

The next day, there was another spitting episode, and I asked Angela to fill the jar again. She didn't enjoy the challenge quite like she did that first day. On day three, there was an episode. Again, I asked Angela to fill the jar. However, being a smart little girl, Angela accidently on purpose dropped the jar, shattering it on the floor. She couldn't contain her grin. Now, there was no jar to fill.

I told Angela not to worry. I went to garage and brought in a shopping bag containing the additional 49 jars. Her smiling face suddenly disappeared. The next day, there were no more episodes, and the 49 other jars were happily used in assorted art projects.

PARENTING

This is Henry. He and his wife Erin have four children which means they have had the "opportunity" to potty train FOUR times over, a daunting task for any parent, but they both admit the first time was the hardest:

When our oldest son was three years old, he showed all the signs of being "ready" to use the potty, so we brought out the little froggy potty and had him sit down.

Nothing happened.

So, we gave him a book for . . . inspiration. Nothing.

So, we did what all good parents do . . . we bribed him. If he used the potty, he would get a toy.

Bingo. He went right away. Toy given, problem solved . . . except that all of a sudden (once the toy was unwrapped), he decided that he really needed his diaper on.

He was done with the potty. Nothing we did could convince him otherwise.

FOUR months went by and we were getting desperate.

As a last ditch effort, one morning we told him there would be no diapers today. That if he was going to use the bathroom, it would be on the floor or in the potty. No exceptions.

He begged until noon for a diaper with the saddest face you ever did see. That's when he started doing the potty dance.

You know the "wiggle" in the step? Bouncing from foot to foot? Our little stinker knew he had to "go," but he wanted a diaper in which to go.

He danced and he danced and he danced. Finally, he could dance no more. There was no holding it back. Luckily, we were ready with the toddler potty and made it just in time.

And wouldn't you know it, when he was done, he informed US that he no longer needed a diaper. He could use the potty. Really?!? Why hadn't we thought of that four months ago?

IS HARD

This is Jessica's family. When their daughter Jessari turned two, Jesica and her husband Merari had her party all planned out. No detail was left to chance, because they knew, as most seasoned parents know, there is nothing more stressful than throwing your kid a birthday party. . . .

In Guatemala, celebrating our children's birthdays is a big deal. All of the immediate family, extended family, and friends are invited. For our oldest daughter Jessari's second birthday, we celebrated at "Fantacilandia" (Fantasyland), a small kids amusement part that specializes in birthdays.

We were all so excited! Everything was planned to perfection. Cakes were made. Special outfits chosen. Invitations were sent. The piñata was stuffed full of candy.

The day of the party came, with much expectation. After we played games, rode rides, and lunch was served, everyone was ready to break open the piñata. With approximately 50 guests in attendance, all eyes were on Jessari, as the birthday girl gets the first swing.

To my dismay, she started screaming at the top of her lungs! She would not hold the piñata stick, nor even get near the piñata. She was clinging onto me for dear life! I was quite embarrassed, trying to make her hit the clown piñata we had purchased especially for her birthday. I felt like everyone was staring at me, and I wanted to crawl into a hole. I was as upset at Jessari for not doing what I thought she should and truth be told a little bit embarrassed at myself for wanting to force her.

It turns out Jessari was afraid of clowns, and we had purchased a clown piñata that was as tall as she was. Birthday party-1, Mommy-0.

This is Sara and her brother, Jeffrey. So cute, aren't they? And that bowtie? Forget about it. But don't let the bowtie fool you. That sweet little blondie could turn a trip to the car wash into an all out war in a matter of seconds…

One time, after an exhausting trip to the grocery story, their mom Lois pulled the family minivan into the garage and started unloading groceries from the trunk. Sara went right into the house (angel baby), but her two-year-old brother stood behind the steering wheel of the van and pretended to drive.

Lois had the keys and thought it would be okay if she stepped inside to put a few bags on the counter. She was gone for seconds when she heard a terrible scraping sound coming from the garage.

She sprinted back only to see the garage door crushing down on top of the trunk of the van. What in the world? Why was it doing that?

She quickly hit the button on the wall and the door started back up, but then it switched and started back down again! She hit the button a second time. The door went up and then back down. Bang, crash, screech, repeat. Bang, crash, screech.

Lois was beside herself. She did not know what to do. Then, as if in slow-motion, she turned to the front of the van and saw that "angel" in the bowtie pushing the garage door button over and over again. It was Jeffery all along!

Later that afternoon, Lois called her husband with the damage report. To her relief, he wasn't mad. He had been foiled by Jeffrey a time or two before himself. He just chuckled to his wife saying, "Guess he really pushed your buttons today!" Haha. Lois was not amused.

IS HARD

IT'S HARD BECAUSE IT IS HARD
AND
IT'S HARD BECAUSE
OTHERS
MAKE IT HARD

Dear Other Mothers,

I am writing to you tonight on a banana-caked keyboard with my hair in pigtails because I am too tired to blow it dry. Forgive me if I get a little fired up, but I feel as though we mothers need an intervention. A no holds barred, all out halt to being each other's worst enemy. For far too long, I have believed that it was just me. That you were right, I was a sub-par parent.

See, I am a mother of a sweet little boy. And yes, we have just the one (And no, I don't know when we're having another, but thank you for asking). My child wasn't even born yet when the snipes started.

When I was in labor and asked for an epidural, my delivery nurse chided me and said, "You know, that can hurt your baby." The next night while desperately trying to breastfeed, another nurse read me a laminated card that said, "Babies must breastfeed for fifteen minutes or be supplemented with formula."

Who reads someone a laminated card ??!!

My baby only ate for nine, so we supplemented with formula. And from then on he refused to eat anything else. He would scream and I would cry wondering how I could fail at something you other mothers did so naturally. Eventually, I gave it up. I told a friend and she said: "You really should be pumping. It's what's best for your baby." *Get new friends*

Hormonal much?

About that. See, I work on a team of guys. (Did I not mention I'm one of those working moms? And yes, I love my job and my child, thanks for asking.) But it is unbelievably awkward to excuse yourself to go pump multiple times throughout the workday. The whole thing overwhelmed me. *True Story.*

And then my baby had reflux. His esophagus literally burned whenever he swallowed milk. We tried everything. We bought special hypoallergenic formula. We had a standing Friday appointment at the pediatrician. Then a nurse practitioner told us, "Try rice cereal in his bottle," so we did. On vacation we bounced him one hour out of every four praying for him to swallow just a few ounces. Later, his pediatric GI told us he was allergic to the rice and we almost lost our religion over that. _Not_ a vacation, that's a trip ☺

But he survived and so did we. Our baby has become a very active, very busy little man who can wear out anyone who tries to keep up with him. Case in point: One day at preschool he was tinkering with an unlatched playground gate and ran into the parking lot. Luckily, his teacher had her running shoes on and scooped him up before anything happened, but we were really upset. I approached the school looking for solutions and instead, a teacher said to me something I'll never forget, "This is going to sound harsh, but he's the ONLY ONE who does this." WHAT!

WHEW!!

This is why we need an intervention. Because what we say to another mother, a young mother, a new mother, matters. She takes it to heart because you can bet she is doing her absolute very best and the last thing she needs is to feel judged by another mom. Challenged? Yes. Encouraged? Absolutely. Given a vacation with umbrella drinks? No brainer. But judged? Never.

So, can we make a pact? Band together like The Beatles (pre-Yoko) and vow never to make another mother feel bad? Never tell her you make home-cooked meals every night when you really just grab nuggets at Chick-fil-A? Never brag to a sleep-deprived mom that your baby has slept through the night at eight weeks with no problems. Never start a sentence with "What you should REALLY do is ____." Listen. Encourage. Cry. Babysit. Those are our communication options. Then maybe we can ALL breathe a collective sigh of relief. And just think of all the money we'll save on therapy. We could get people to clean our houses.

Signed,

A Mother

Dream on!

Reminds me of Tina Fey!

"When people say, 'You really really must' do something, it means you don't really have to. No one ever says, 'You really really must deliver the baby during labor.' When it's true, it doesn't need to be said!!!"

There's an ancient story about a cupbearer named Nehemiah who led a small band of workers to rebuild the wall of Jerusalem. The wall had been destroyed by insurgents, and the gates were burned with fire. This was the city of Nehemiah's ancestors, his family, so it was personal. With the king's permission, Nehemiah and the people worked day and night to rebuild; it is said that they "worked with their whole hearts."

But enemies encircled them, looking to distract Nehemiah and destroy the progress on the wall. One day, they sent a message to Nehemiah to come outside and meet them. Nehemiah replied, "I am doing a **GREAT WORK** and I cannot come down."

Four times the enemy sent their message and ALL four times, Nehemiah gave them the same response. He stayed focused on the task he believed God gave him, and the wall was built in a record 52 days.

Might the same be said about parenting? That it, too, is a **GREAT WORK**.

Pastor Andy Stanley and his wife, Sandra, talk about the need for guardrails around our time as parents. Sandra said she had to tell herself: "There are just some categories of things that I am not going to be able to do for now, for this season. I need to be focused on the main thing that God is calling me to do for right now, and the other things are going to have to wait."

She's right, there will always be distractions—**good things**, like phone calls and emails and bosses who want us to work late; Facebook news feeds to check and friends who want to have coffee. But we cannot apologize or marginalize the work it takes to be a good parent—to mold a child's character, teaching them to follow a God who loves them.

We must be brave enough to say NO to the good in order to make room for the great. We must whisper over and over to ourselves **"I am doing a great work and I cannot come down."**

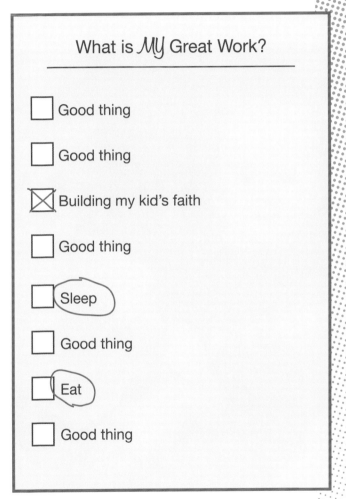

What is *MY* Great Work?

☐ Good thing

☐ Good thing

☒ Building my kid's faith

☐ Good thing

☐ Sleep

☐ Good thing

☐ Eat

☐ Good thing

A scene from "Friends" – When Phoebe told her brother and his wife they were having triplets. (Phoebe was their surrogate.)

Phoebe: Oh, well, okay. Hey, y'know how when you're umm, you're walking down the street and you see three people in a row, and you say, "Oh, that's nice"?

Frank: Yes.

Phoebe: Okay, yeah well, good news. You're going to have three babies.

Alice: Three babies?

Frank: I finally got my band!

Alice: We're gonna have a big family; I've always wanted a big family!

Phoebe: I'm so glad you guys are happy, I was so afraid you were going to be all freaked.

Frank: Why would we be freaked?

Phoebe: No, no, maybe 'cause it's harder to raise them, and the added expense, and. . . .

Frank: (They're less than happy now) Oh.

Alice: Right.

Phoebe: No, back to happy. Back to happy!

Alice: No-no-no, no, it's going to be fine. Because umm, because I teach Home Ec, and uh, I can have 30 kids making baby clothes all year long. Y'know. It'll-it'll be like my very own little sweatshop.

Frank: Yeah, I've been thinking ever since you said we were having triplets, the best thing for me to do is to drop out of college and get a job.

Alice: No, Frank.

Phoebe: No, you can't quit college! No! You're in college? Really?

Frank: Yeah, refrigerator college.

Alice: Yeah.

Frank: Yeah, y'know, when we found out we were going to have a baby, y'know, I figured, y'know, like I should, y'know, have like a career—and I love refrigerators!

Phoebe: You can't give up on your dream.

Frank: No, it's okay. We're-we're gonna have three kids! And that's-that's a different kind of dream.
Three kids and no money.

HAVE YOU EVER WONDERED

how to help them become great?

This is Beckham. He spends more time IN timeout than OUT.

Greg is terrified of public restrooms. He will not go in them.

Hannah sucks on her stuffed animals every night while she sleeps.

Sarah likes to put things up her nose - marbles, blueberries, and six-inch noodles.

Luke freaks out if different foods touch on the plate. He makes his mom take the offending pieces away before he can eat again.

Annie refuses to wear anything but dresses that spin. If they don't spin, they don't go on Annie.

(These stories are real but the names have been changed to protect these kids from future embarrassment.)

And So Did These People...

Can you guess who?

This sixth president of the United States swam naked regularly in the Potomac River at 5 a.m.

This legendary baseball player wore a cabbage leaf under his cap to keep him cool. He changed it every two innings.

This legendary scientist couldn't speak really well until after he was nine years old.

This president of the United States went to school for less than a year. He taught himself to read and write.

This famous children's author did not like to have children in his own home.

This famous entrepreneur was afraid of mice.

These people are real and their names have not been changed because they are more successful than you or I might ever hope to be and would have nothing to be embarrassed about—if they were still alive and reading this book.

ANSWERS: Albert Einstein, John Adams, Babe Ruth, Abraham Lincoln, Dr. Seuss, Walt Disney

**Insert
your child's
photo here**

Be Them!

"100 years from now, the only thing that will matter is someone's relationship with God."

The best person to help your child know how
to have a relationship with God is YOU.

But don't get
overwhelmed

Because these people

want to partner with you.

Start with the Basics

1. God Made Me

2. God Loves Me

3. Jesus Wants To Be My Friend Forever

USE WHAT YOU H VE

Play Time

use their toys to act out any Bible story

Bath Time

remind them that God made them fantastic

Drive Time

talk about the world God made as they watch out the window

This cheery board book is the perfect introduction to nursery rhymes. Children will meet Humpty Dumpty, Little Miss Muffet, Old King Cole, and other beloved characters, illustrated with warmth

Cuddle Time

read a Bible story together and pray

The other night, three-year-old Levi was sitting at dinner with his whole extended family when someone said, kind of off the cuff, "Hey Levi, Auntie Dar's leg is still hurting, we'll have to pray for her." And to everyone's surprise, Levi bowed his head right there and said: "Dear God, please help Auntie Dar's leg (cue all adults frantically bowing their heads). In Jesus' name, Amen."

Four-year-old Jared just had to have a chest X-ray, and he was very brave. Afterwards, he asked the X-ray techs if he could see the X-ray. They showed him and he just stared at it. They pointed to each bone and shape and told him what they were. Later when he got in the van to go home, his mom asked him what he thought about seeing his insides? And Jared said, "God made me!"

Four-year-old Emerson had to weather some big thunderstorms last night. In the morning, her mommy asked her if the storms woke her up. "Yes," Emerson replied, "but I remembered what Mr. John said in church. "If thunder comes and you're scared, don't worry because God is there to help you."

Three-year-old twin brothers, Nicholas and Zachary, chattered all the way home from church about what they had learned—that God loves them! When they got home, Zachary started crying and Nicholas went to him, laid on the floor with him and said, "It's okay, God loves you."

HAVE YOU EVER WONDERED

what your story will be?

We all hold pictures of what we think a family is "supposed" to be.

But there is no perfect picture.

God wants to show His love
through real families like YOURS !

Insert
your family
photo here

God wants to write a bigger story
through your family...

...so that your children can see His grace and goodness.

This is Rachel. Like most high school girls, she planned to graduate, go to college, get a job, someday meet the right guy and then get married. But somewhere during her junior year, life got confusing, and Rachel got lost. After a series of wrong turns, she found herself alone and pregnant at age 17.

Overwhelmed and anxious, she dropped out of school and tried to cope with what was happening to her life. How in the world had she gotten here?

So many emotions churned inside of her. Anger. She was mad, really, really mad at herself. Disappointment. Each day brought such difficult and heart-wrenching conversations with people she cared about. Fear. How would she ever navigate the future with a baby?

Deep down inside, Rachel also questioned her faith. God had been part of her childhood growing up, but she wondered how He felt about her life right now. Could God still love someone who had messed up—made the wrong choice? Would He hold a grudge? Not answer her prayers? Those thoughts haunted her daily.

Rachel's questions led her down the path where she discovered grace—the undeserved kind of grace available for all of us when we make mistakes. It comes from a heavenly Father who never stops loving one of his children. As she gave birth to her son Aden, she started to understand that kind of love. There wasn't any part of her that didn't love her son. Could God love her even more than that?

The most difficult part of becoming a mother wasn't the birth itself. It was forgiving herself. That took time. And a supportive family. And, a best friend who wouldn't let her give up on the road up ahead.

So, what does her story look like five years later?

Aden is a happy five-year-old getting ready to start Kindergarten this fall. Rachel just finished Cosmetology school and is ready to become a hair stylist. And, a few months from now, Rachel is getting married to a man she met at church. Her friends say this guy is "great" for her and Aden.

Through a really difficult journey, Rachel discovered the wonder of a God who delights in giving second chances, and she can't wait for the next chapter in her story to begin.

BIGGER STORY

This is Tina, Sam and her son, Myles. Tina's story is one of a nightmare many families live, but reading it will give you so much hope. It's better if she tells it:

My son, Myles, started off like most kids. Alert. Curious. Happy. Around 18 months old, that all changed. Smiles had disappeared. Laughing was gone. And, maybe hardest of all, his words went away. It had been subtle. Insidious. Like a little bit of him had been stolen from us every night, leaving him more solemn, more silent every morning.

As we searched for answers, there was one I hoped we wouldn't find: Autism. But that was the answer, and it only raised the most painful questions my husband and I had ever asked ourselves. Questions about his future. Questions about the quality of his life.

Myles seemed to be trapped in this cave, all alone, beyond our reach. He didn't respond to his name, seemed to find it difficult to even look into our eyes, and it was often like we didn't even exist. I missed the child he had been becoming—the one who laughed and called me Mommy. And for the next three years, his silence was deafening.

We tried every therapy and medicine and natural remedy we could find that might help. I was so discouraged most days. And then, I'll never forget. Myles was five years old. He hadn't said much for a long time, and he definitely hadn't called me Mommy since he was about a year and a half. I think I was washing dishes. I know I was in the kitchen, and then I heard it. So soft, I thought it was my imagination.

Mommy.

I turned around and there Myles stood, looking me right in my eyes. Calling me mommy. My response was melodramatic, and probably slightly frightening to my mostly silent five-year-old. I literally dropped to my knees in front of him and grabbed him so hard it may have hurt. And I just cried. That day was light in the dark for me.

It's why I started a foundation, Myles-A-Part. I believe our family experienced this because God knew we would feel burdened to help our son AND others. His story is now part of a solution for other families through the funds we raise to assist them. As we see the progress these children make, we will be a part of their success. Their stories will become ours. That makes my heart swell with pride and possibility for us all.

This is April. She and her husband, Brian, had what they called "Plan A." They were going to start a family. But after trying for nearly three years to get pregnant, enduring a brutally hard, indescribably painful journey through fertility treatments, the little blue plus sign they had desperately longed to see would not come. They needed a new plan.

So, they turned to another dream, adoption. They had always talked about adopting from Ethiopia, but didn't realize that maybe this was God's "Plan A" for them all along—His timing, not theirs; His strength made perfect in our weakness. So, they started the process, the one where you fill out papers and pray and stress eat while holding your breath, waiting for the day someone tells you that you can bring your children home. Well, two years later, the day finally came and they were granted adoption of two little ones, Judah, 2.5 years old and 11-month-old, Addise.

They felt blissfully happy. Complete. Whole. The old dream of having biological children had all but disappeared. And they knew Judah and Addise were indisputably God's Plan A for their family.

But the twists and turns were just beginning. Nine months after they brought their kiddos home, April and Brian found out they were pregnant. They found themselves in absolute shock—and simultaneously terrified. Becoming parents to three kids under four in 18 months. They would need new cars, a new home, and a new strategy for survival. They found themselves, once again, having to surrender their plans to God, and it was not easy.

"Very little of this pregnancy makes sense to me," writes April. "The past couple of weeks have involved a LOT of tears, Tums, careful eating, desperate prayers, silent fears, but God is proving He is a God of miracles and humor."

This might not have been their "Plan A," or their "Plan B" but April and Brian are trusting in a God who directs their steps and reshapes their plans, knowing that if God is control, then "Plan A 3.0" might be pretty awesome. (Once the morning sickness stops!)

This is Chris and his beautiful family. The baby in the middle is Hallie. At her 14-week ultrasound, she was diagnosed with Trisomy 13, a devastating disease that meant if Hallie made it to term, she would only live a few short hours, days or perhaps a handful of weeks Chris and Katie, like we all would be, were heartbroken.

Hallie was born on December 19, and her story captured the hearts of thousands of friends and family. People posted pictures on Facebook holding "Hope for Hallie" signs, and on day five of her life, her daddy wrote a message on their blog:

Thank you to everyone, for your prayers and support, they have meant so much to us. But I've got to be honest, when I first saw the signs and hashtags labeled 'Hope for Hallie,' I was a little nervous. I guess I wanted to make sure people knew what to hope for. The prayers for a miracle of full recovery in Hallie's health have been a braver prayer than I honestly was willing to pray. Probably out of the fear that God might not 'fix' her. I also didn't want to assume that Hallie's health was the indicator of God's goodness to us. We've seen God's goodness in so many ways, and greatly through each of you. The bottom line is this: Please don't hinge your willingness to believe in God on Hallie's survival.

The reality is, she won't.

I want to follow that horrible sentence with this. Hallie's survival was never our 'Hope for Hallie.' We knew the day we heard the words 'Trisomy 13,' Hallie's life would be short, and maybe just hours/days if she survived birth. Our

'Hope for Hallie' is that people would see life as a gift, and draw near to God. Based on your outpouring of love and support, I would say: Mission accomplished. More people know Hallie's name within the last five days than will know my name throughout my entire life. Please don't feel sorry for Hallie—or us.

We will continue to enjoy every moment we are given with Hallie. We're heartbroken. Extremely heartbroken. We cry—probably hourly. God's purpose for Hallie does not exempt us from the pain of losing her. Don't be misled into thinking we're all laughing and celebrating all of the time.

Hallie is perfectly-made for us. She has a cleft lip and palette, no eyes, and we're pretty sure she's deaf. But she's still perfect to us. Her soul shines through her.

Finally, I'll leave you with a shot taken last night shortly after we arrived home from the hospital. One of our 'Hope for Hallie' participants went to Bass Pro Shop to do some family photos with Santa. She was holding a 'Hope for Hallie' sign in the photo. Santa asked about it, and was moved by our story. He wanted to help bring some Christmas cheer to our family. And—at 9 p.m. last

night, after working a strenuous, all-day schedule, he drove the 30 miles south to our home to make us smile.

This single act of selflessness and love has got to be a top-three moment for me in my life. I would compare it to the "Move that bus!" Extreme Home Makeover emotion. Incredible. He brought gifts for our girls and us, prayed for our family, and then lead us all in "Silent Night." Santa, thank you for honoring our family in such a sacrificial way. (I see God's love all over this.)

Sweet little Hallie went to be with Jesus at 12:30 a.m. on Christmas Eve.

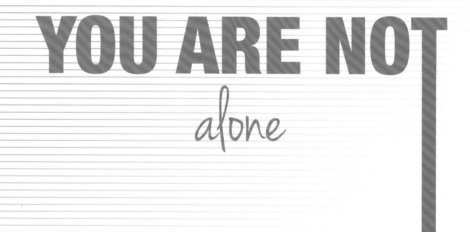

YOU ARE NOT *alone*

Remember, God is doing a great work in _YOU_ too.

And YOUR story is not over yet.

But this book is.

The End.

A special thank you to the following families for sharing their pictures and their stories with us.

Alvir Family	McMurtry Family
Arnold Family	Nunes Family
Boughey Family	Pallansch Family
Bowie Family	Panuganti Family
Carroll Family	Phenix Family
DeJesus Family	Roach Family
Delich Family	Roberts Family
Diaz Family	Rowell Famiy
Dula Family	Roy Family
Galema Family	Schlabach Family
Gatlin Family	Springer Family
Green Family	Tamborello Family
Hill Family	Templeton Family
Hogan Family	T. Walker Family
Ivy Family	M. Walker Family
Kent Family	Wilburn Family
Kinyanjui Family	Williams Family
MacDonald Family	Woodall Family
McKee Family	Zonio Family

We couldn't have done this without you!